MARGRET & H.A.REY'S
Curious George
Says Thank You

Written by Emily Flaschner Meyer and Julie M. Bartynski

Illustrated in the style of H. A. Rey by Anna Grossnickle Hines

HOUGHTON MIFFLIN HARCOURT

Boston   New York   2011

For my parents, Dan and Wendy — I can't thank you enough!
—E.F.M.

For my wonderful parents, John and Shirley
—J.M.B.

For Violet
—A.G.H.

www.hmhbooks.com
www.curiousgeorge.com
The text of this book is set in Adobe Garamond.
The illustrations are watercolors.

ISBN 978-0-547-86339-9 HC
ISBN 978-0-547-81852-8 PA

Printed in Mexico
RDT 10 9 8 7 6 5 4
4500411461

This is George.
He was a good little monkey and always very curious.
Today George received a surprise in the mail. "It looks like you got a card, George," said the man with the yellow hat.

It was a thank-you card from George's neighbor Betsy.

Dear George,
Thank you so much for
the birthday present.
I'm putting the stickers
you gave me on every-
thing. Even this card!
Sincerely,
Betsy

The card made George smile. It also made him curious. Who could he give a thank-you card to? George thought and thought.

He could send one to the science museum director, Dr. Lee, who had shown George her favorite collection of dinosaur fossils. Of course, there was also the librarian who helped him pick out books. Hmm . . . The store clerk at the market always saved the best bananas for him. And his friend Bill let George fly his kite in the park.

George had so many people to thank—he had to get started right away!
First he gathered paper, envelopes, crayons, and stickers.
Then he got to work.

The man with the yellow hat walked in to find George covered from head to toe.

"Uh-oh, George! What are you doing?"

George held up Betsy's card and pointed to the papers
scattered around him.
"Oh, I see, George," said his friend. "You're making your
own thank-you cards. What a nice idea. Would you like
some help?"

The man wrote while George decorated. George was having so much fun that they even made a stack of extra cards. "We can hand-deliver these tomorrow. Everyone will be happy to see you, George."

Their first stop was the science museum.
"George, it's so good to see you," said Dr. Lee. "What a lovely card! I'm going to hang it in my office right now."

Next they stopped at the library. "What a great card," the librarian said. "I'm going to set it here on my desk where everyone can see it. George, we have some new books in the children's section that you might like, if you have time." George looked at his friend. "All right," the man said. "I will go get a book for myself."

George noticed the mail carrier leaving the library. She was the one who had brought George his thank-you card in the first place. He wanted to give her one of his cards too! George hurried out the door. Could he catch her in time?

George jumped up and down on the steps, waving a card, but a group of children was just getting off a bus. They were coming to the library for story hour. George couldn't see which way the mail carrier had gone.

But, oh! There was a streetlight nearby. George was curious.
Maybe if he climbed it, he could see where the mail carrier
was going.

George started to climb the streetlight as fast as only a monkey can. But when he was halfway up the pole, his bag slipped off.

In an instant, all of George's thank-you cards went
whirling through the air.
Oh, no! How would George deliver his cards now?

George slid down the pole and grabbed at the cards swirling around him.

A boy looked up. "Hey! It's snowing mail!"

A little girl said, "Don't worry, little monkey. We'll help you pick up your cards."

The children gathered up the cards. George was very grateful for their help. He was also grateful that he had brought extra cards. He decided to give them to all of the children. "These cards are so nice!" said the teacher.

The man with the yellow hat came hurrying down the steps. "George! I didn't see you leave. It looks like you've had quite an adventure out here."

The man thanked the teacher and his students for helping George.

"Let's finish delivering those thank-you cards," said the man. George and his friend stopped by the market and the park and then headed home.

George felt a little sad that he hadn't caught up to the mail carrier. But wait! Who was that at George's house?

and the man went into

ial thank-you card

George proudly gave her a thank-you card.
"Wow, George!" said the mail carrier. "I'm usually
the one delivering the cards. This sure is a treat!"